Why Activate?

It's widely recognised that self-regulated learners are more effective learners. For example, in England, the Education Endowment Foundation suggests that 'metacognition and self-regulation' are among the most impactful things a school can focus on, providing 'very high impact for very low cost based on extensive evidence' (Education Endowment Foundation, n.d.). However, teachers and leaders are often unsure precisely what 'metacognition and self-regulation' means – or what these ideas look like in practice.

Clearly, if it's possible for teachers to 'activate' children and young people to become the drivers of their own learning, then there's a strong case for doing so. This resource has been designed to enable time-pressed teachers, leaders and support staff to understand the theory and practice of self-regulated learning in an accessible way. Working your way through the activities in this professional learning resource will increase your ability to realise the potential of these powerful ideas to improve outcomes for children and young people while enhancing the development of your own self-regulated learning.

What is Activate?

Activate is a card-based professional learning resource which supports teachers, leaders and support staff to promote self-regulated learning. The resource has been developed by specialists at the UCL Centre for Educational Leadership, in conjunction with colleagues from the global schools group, Cognita. Drawing on research into self-regulated learning, professional learning and leadership, Activate helps schools to explore the following questions:

- What do the terms metacognition, self-regulation and self-regulated learning mean – and what do they look like in practice for teachers, leaders and pupils?
- How can teachers develop their teaching practice so that pupils become more effective, proactive, self-regulated learners?
- How can leaders support teachers to try out new approaches in collaboration with others?
- How can teachers and leaders evaluate the impact of changed practice on pupil learning?
- How can teachers and leaders develop their own self-regulated learning?
- How can teachers and leaders refine their practice and embed professional learning so that it is shared and sustained over time?

In this guide, we begin by exploring what we mean by self-regulated learning and its relationship with metacognition and self-regulation. Next, we introduce you to the Activate resource and the professional learning process that underpins it, and explain how you can use Activate to promote self-regulated learning among teachers, leaders and pupils in your school(s). In the Annexes, we include an extended explanation of the conceptual framework that underpins Activate, some examples of particular techniques for developing aspects of self-regulated learning, and further details about our approach to professional learning and learning conversations. We also include references and a bibliography of key articles and texts in the field.

Self-regulated learning

Activate is designed to help teachers, leaders and pupils become more confident, proactive, self-regulated learners. In order to understand self-regulated learning, we need a clear understanding of two key concepts: metacognition and self-regulation. We define these terms as follows:

Metacognition: Monitoring and controlling your thought processes.

Self-regulation: Monitoring and controlling your feelings and behaviours.

We can see that these ideas mirror one another in that they both involve monitoring and controlling. We define monitoring and controlling as follows:

Monitoring: Paying attention to your thoughts, feelings and/or behaviours. This can involve noticing, observing or tracking over time. Through developing self-awareness, you learn how to control your thoughts, feelings and behaviours.

Controlling: Managing your own learning – for example, by setting goals, managing distractions or trying new strategies. Learning to control your thoughts, feelings and behaviours is essential to becoming a more confident, self-regulated learner.

The difference between metacognition and self-regulation is that metacognition is about monitoring and controlling your internal thought processes, whereas self-regulation is about monitoring and controlling how you interact with the external world through your feelings (physical or emotional) and behaviours.

Because they are related to thoughts, feelings and behaviours, it is clear that metacognition and self-regulation are broad concepts that extend beyond learning. To apply these powerful ideas to education, we use the concept of self-regulated learning. We define this as follows:

Self-regulated learning: Applying metacognition and self-regulation to your learning.

Figure 1 shows how these ideas relate to one another.

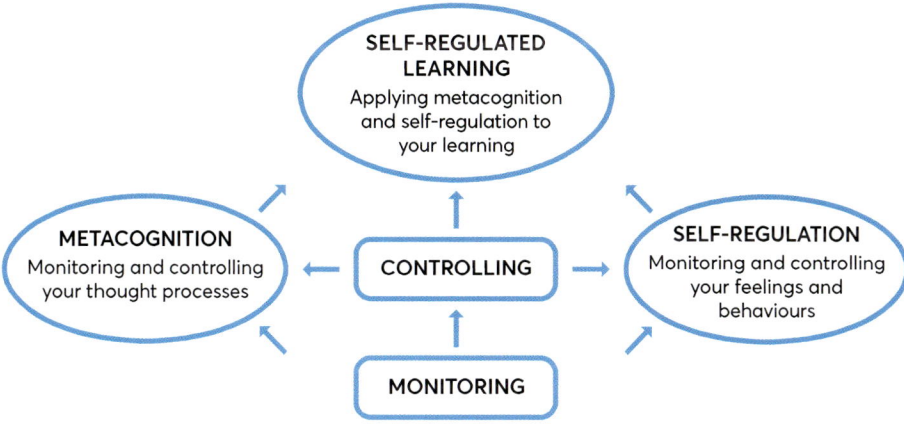

Figure 1. Metacognition, self-regulation and self-regulated learning

Here, we can see that the process of self-regulated learning begins with *monitoring* your thoughts, feelings and behaviours. Through doing this, an individual can gain an increasing awareness of how they respond to certain situations – and of the choices they can make in *controlling* how they respond to those situations in the future.

As with all models, the scheme outlined in Figure 1 is a simplified version of reality. Additional factors influence the extent to which a pupil is willing or able to regulate their own learning. In **Activate**, we suggest that there are five enabling factors that help pupils to become more confident, proactive, self-regulated learners. These are:

Knowledge: This can include knowledge of tasks, strategies, self and others, as well as knowledge of subjects. Connected knowledge leads to deep understanding.

Self-efficacy: Believing that you can be successful when carrying out a specific task, studying a particular topic, or developing the habits and skills of self-regulated learning.

Motivation: Being enthusiastic about doing something. Motivation can be intrinsic (coming from within you) or extrinsic (inspired by external rewards or consequences). Self-regulated learners are skilled at motivating themselves to learn.

Oracy: Speaking and listening effectively in a range of contexts. This includes having productive dialogue in pairs and small groups, as well as being confident and articulate in different situations.

Agency: Taking ownership over your own learning. It is linked to ideas of autonomy, independence and choice. By definition, self-regulated learning requires a degree of learner agency.

Pulling together these ideas, you can see a visual representation of the **Activate** conceptual framework in Figure 2.

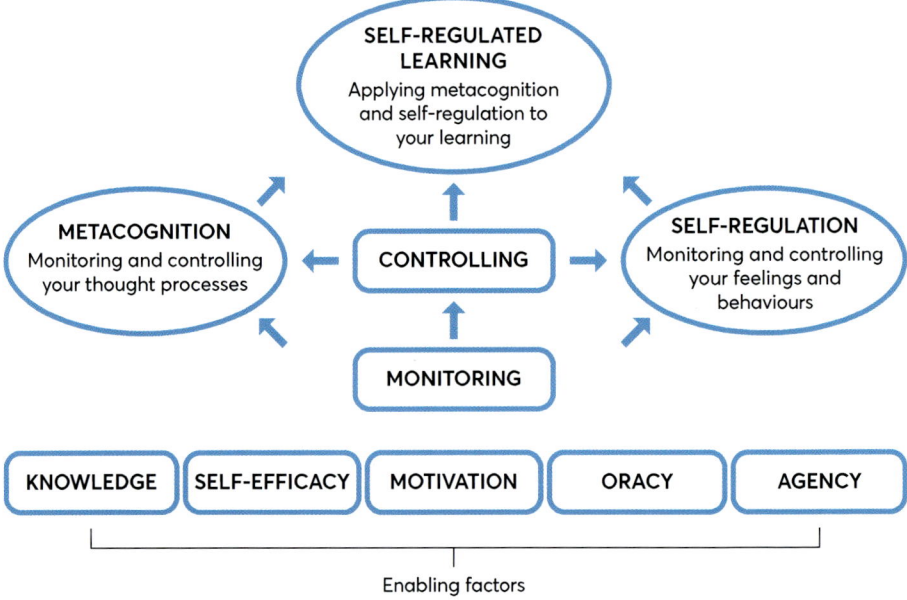

Figure 2. The **Activate** conceptual framework

The **Activate** resource is designed to help young people become more effective, self-regulated learners through learning how to monitor and control their thoughts, feelings and behaviours.

In addition, **Activate** is intended to help young people develop the five 'enabling factors' that underpin self-regulated learning. In particular, learning about the theory and practice of self-regulated learning enables and encourages young people to:

- Deepen their understanding of subjects, self-regulated learning and themselves (knowledge).
- Believe that they can become more confident, proactive, self-regulated learners (self-efficacy).
- Become more energised and enthusiastic about leading their own learning (motivation).
- Communicate their thoughts, feelings and behaviours with their teachers and peers (oracy).
- Make meaningful choices about what they learn, when and how (agency).

In Annex 1, you will find a more detailed explanation of the conceptual framework that underpins **Activate**.

How Activate helps pupils regulate their thoughts, feelings and behaviours

When using Activate, a pupil might notice that they tend to engage in negative self-talk about maths – that they will 'never be any good' at it, or that they 'hate' it (feelings). They might notice a tendency to catastrophise about what might happen if they raise their hand to answer a question – that 'I'll probably get it wrong' or that 'everyone will laugh at me' (thoughts). As a consequence, that pupil never raises their hand in maths lessons, and averts their eyes whenever the teacher asks a question (behaviours).

Through noticing patterns about their thoughts, feelings and behaviours, the pupil can start to change how they relate to maths as a subject. For example, they might undertake a 'reframing' activity, in which they 'flip the script' and start to tell themselves a different story – that they will be good at maths one day, as long as they are prepared to take risks and learn from their mistakes.

Through this process, the pupil will be able to make different decisions about how they behave in maths lessons in the future. If they notice that they are engaging in negative self-talk again, they can 'flip the script' and remind themselves that a different story might actually be true. They might start to answer questions in maths lessons. If they get something wrong, they might find that it isn't so bad – nobody laughed at them, and they learnt from the experience. And if they receive positive feedback, this will provide evidence that the different story they told themselves is coming true. This in turn will further influence their thoughts, feelings and behaviours about maths in the future.

Promoting self-regulated learning through Activate

The Activate theory of change

The design of Activate is underpinned by a theory of change. A theory of change is a diagram showing your theory – or story – of how you plan to bring about change: an explanation of why certain things happen (see, for example, Taplin and Clark, 2012; Harries et al., 2014). The diagram maps the final intended impact you want to have – your ultimate outcome. It also sets out what changes are necessary for this impact to come about – your intermediate outcomes, as well as the actions you are taking to promote these outcomes. The Activate theory of change (see Figure 3) emphasises the importance of focusing professional learning on both teachers and leaders in bringing about successful schoolwide change related to self-regulated learning.

Looking at it sequentially, working left to right, the **Activate** theory of change is as follows: using **Professional Learning** and **Leadership Learning** cards, teachers and leaders will develop research understanding and learning processes that will change their beliefs, knowledge and understanding, and behaviours (sometimes described as intermediate outcomes). This in turn will enable pupils to become more confident, proactive, self-regulated learners. An extended description is available as a downloadable resource.

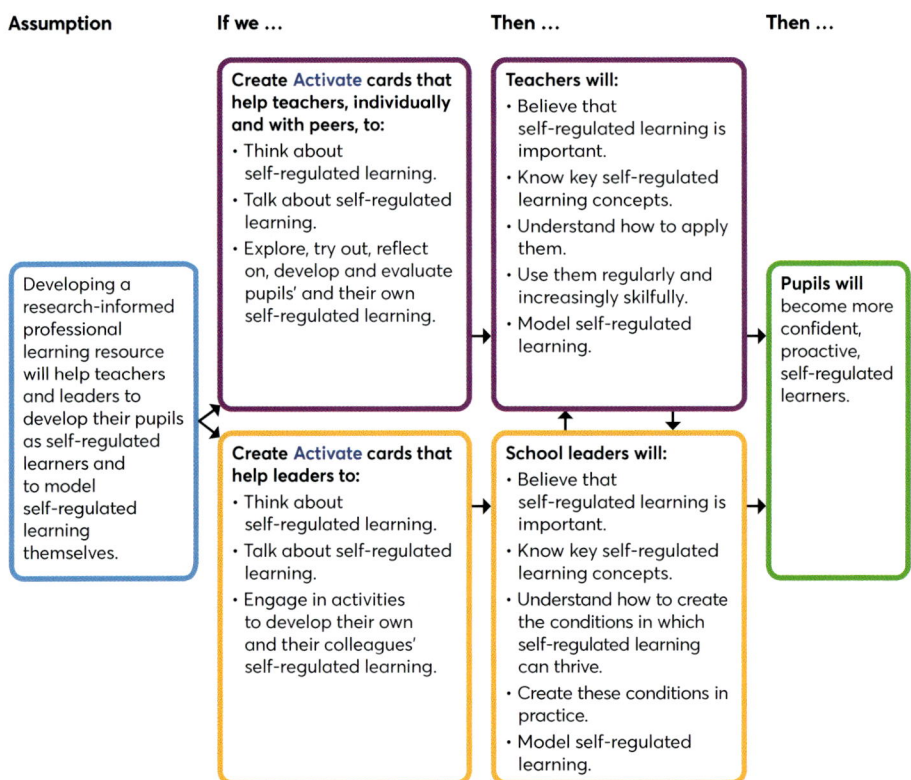

Assumption	If we …	Then …	Then …
Developing a research-informed professional learning resource will help teachers and leaders to develop their pupils as self-regulated learners and to model self-regulated learning themselves.	**Create Activate cards that help teachers, individually and with peers, to:** • Think about self-regulated learning. • Talk about self-regulated learning. • Explore, try out, reflect on, develop and evaluate pupils' and their own self-regulated learning.	**Teachers will:** • Believe that self-regulated learning is important. • Know key self-regulated learning concepts. • Understand how to apply them. • Use them regularly and increasingly skilfully. • Model self-regulated learning.	**Pupils will** become more confident, proactive, self-regulated learners.
	Create Activate cards that help leaders to: • Think about self-regulated learning. • Talk about self-regulated learning. • Engage in activities to develop their own and their colleagues' self-regulated learning.	**School leaders will:** • Believe that self-regulated learning is important. • Know key self-regulated learning concepts. • Understand how to create the conditions in which self-regulated learning can thrive. • Create these conditions in practice. • Model self-regulated learning.	

*Figure 3. The **Activate** theory of change*

The Activate cards

There are six sets of cards connected to different aspects of the **Activate** theory of change. These are grouped into two sets of three cards.

Self-regulated learning cards (smaller)

- **Key Concept** – these turquoise cards define the key concepts involved in self-regulated learning, as outlined in the conceptual framework (Figure 2 on page 6). There are five *overarching concepts* – metacognition, self-regulation, self-regulated learning, monitoring and controlling – and five *enabling factors* – knowledge, self-efficacy, motivation, oracy and agency.
- **Pupil Action** – these green cards exemplify the characteristics of self-regulated learners and are framed using the types of questions that they will ultimately ask themselves.
- **Teacher Action** – these purple cards suggest a number of tried and tested techniques and strategies that teachers can use to promote self-regulated learning. Some of these cards also refer to fuller descriptions found in the downloadable resources.

Professional learning and leadership learning cards (larger)

- **Professional Learning** – these purple cards contain activities using the small **Key Concept**, **Pupil Action** and **Teacher Action** cards to help teachers learn how to promote and model self-regulated learning.
- **Leadership Learning** – these gold cards contain activities using the **Key Concept**, **Pupil Action** and **Teacher Action** cards to help leaders learn how to develop the conditions

that promote self-regulated learning and how to model self-regulated learning themselves.

● **Teacher Scenario** and **Leadership Scenario** – these cards provide examples of learning experiences that promote self-regulated learning, and outline some of the challenges faced by teachers and leaders in trying to develop self-regulated learning.

The **Activate** professional learning cycle

In using **Activate**, you will follow a professional learning cycle, shown in Figure 4. Starting with familiarising yourself with the concepts underpinning self-regulated learning, this inquiry cycle draws on extensive research (by the authors and others – see Annex 2 and References and bibliography) into professional learning, the leadership of professional learning and the practice of teaching.

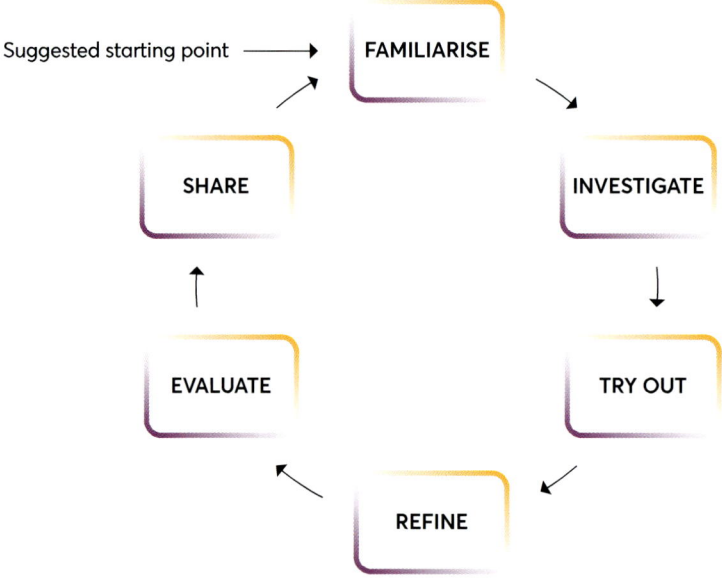

*Figure 4. The **Activate** professional learning cycle*

For each phase of the inquiry cycle there is one **Professional Learning** and one **Leadership Learning** card, except for **FAMILIARISE**, which has two **Professional Learning** cards and one **Leadership Learning** card. Each card contains several activities. These can be completed in any order, although we sometimes make suggestions to help sequence learning. The **Professional Learning** and **Leadership Learning** activities model the principles of self-regulated learning, enabling teachers and leaders to engage with the **Key Concept** cards and consider how to bring these to life using the ideas from the **Teacher Action**, **Pupil Action**, **Leadership Scenario** and **Teacher Scenario** cards.

The **Activate** professional learning cycle is designed to bring about sustained improvements to self-regulated learning within and across schools by developing the practice of teachers and leaders in three dimensions:

- Depth of learning, rooted in research and evidence.

- Breadth of learning, to ensure that the development of self-regulated learning is widespread.

- Length of learning, to ensure that improvements to self-regulated learning are embedded and continue into the future.

The six phases in the **Activate** professional learning cycle are: **FAMILIARISE**, **INVESTIGATE**, **TRY OUT**, **REFINE**, **EVALUATE** and **SHARE**.

- **FAMILIARISE** – These initial activities help you to explore each **Key Concept** and its meaning, along with the pupil and teacher actions associated with self-regulated learning. They enable you to start with the end in mind – to get clear about what successful self-regulated learning looks like in practice. You can also use the **FAMILIARISE** cards in the **REFINE** phase to revisit the key concepts as your understanding of how they relate to one another develops and deepens over time.

- **INVESTIGATE** – These activities help you to explore your current context in relation to self-regulated learning. Through a process of inquiry involving self-reflection, auditing, questioning and observing, you will examine what self-regulated learning looks like in your context and consider how you can develop it further. The **INVESTIGATE** phase also involves exploring new approaches to promoting self-regulated learning, which you may choose to put into practice during the **TRY OUT** phase.

- **TRY OUT** – These activities encourage you to experiment with new practices in order to develop the conditions for self-regulated learning. They involve checking in with critical friends, seeking and receiving feedback, and adapting self-regulated learning practices to your context.

- **REFINE** – These activities enable you to develop and deepen your practice through greater challenge, further reflection and feedback as you hone and sharpen your practice, deepen your understanding and develop your adaptive expertise (see References and bibliography) in promoting self-regulated learning.

- **EVALUATE** – These activities focus on checking progress, determining what difference efforts to promote and develop self-regulated learning are making and evaluating the impact of changes to practice on teacher and pupil outcomes.

- **SHARE** – These activities ensure that new knowledge, understandings, beliefs and effective practices for developing self-regulated learning are widely shared and become embedded throughout the school and your wider networks.

Learning conversations

Learning conversations are at the heart of **Activate**'s professional learning processes. The **Activate** cards are designed to encourage and facilitate learning conversations and associated actions. For us, learning conversations are how educators make meaning together, jointly coming up with new insights and knowledge. Such dialogue stimulates reflection that challenges thinking in ways that help people create new knowledge and lead to intentional change to enhance practice and pupil learning (Stoll, 2012). You will find dialogue points throughout the **Professional Learning** and **Leadership Learning** cards. To find out more about stimulating learning conversations, see Annex 3.

Using Activate

Who can use Activate?

Activate can be used by a range of staff in one or several schools, including:

- Leaders (middle and teacher leaders, senior leaders, head teachers/principals, system leaders, network and hub leaders).
- Teachers (experienced teachers, early career teachers, trainees).
- Support staff (special educational needs and disabilities co-ordinators, learning support assistants, teaching assistants and others).
- Governors and trustees.

The **Professional Learning** cards are primarily aimed at teachers working together in groups – such as subject, phase or year groups – and we use the term 'teacher' in the **Activate** cards. However, those teams may also include support staff and other specialists who would benefit from being involved in some of the activities.

The **Leadership Learning** cards can be used by teams of senior leaders, system leaders, middle leaders, teacher leaders or a combination of these, within or across schools. They can also be used by pairs of teachers, or teachers and leaders, to stimulate professional learning conversations and could be used as a coaching resource.

Activate isn't differentiated to meet the needs of different age groups, demographics or cultures. This is an intentional design feature: the resource is designed to provide teachers and pupils across different schools and countries with a shared understanding of what self-regulated learning means in theory, and to share some examples of what it can look like in practice. However, professional learning resources are most impactful when they are adapted by practitioners to suit the needs of their particular context, rather than being taken off the shelf and implemented in a uniform way. Teachers and leaders in schools know their setting, their colleagues and their pupils best. We therefore encourage you to adapt these ideas and practices to suit the environment in which you work. In doing so, you will be modelling some of the key concepts involved in self-regulated learning.

Engaging with Activate

There are several ways of engaging with **Activate**. We suggest that teachers and leaders seeking to promote self-regulated learning consider the ideas below and explore the resource with a small, representative group of leaders and staff before introducing it more widely. **Activate** can be used for various purposes over different time frames.

Short term (i.e. a week to a term):
- To enable individual teachers to identify priorities at the start of a school year.
- To support (peer) coaching or mentoring conversations around a particular issue.
- To inform lesson study or peer observations.

Medium term (i.e. a year to two years):
- To support the implementation of a department or phase improvement/development plan.
- To enable teachers to deepen their practice through practitioner inquiry.
- To support target setting and review progress in performance reviews.

Long term (i.e. three years or more):
- To support the development of a three- to five-year whole-school improvement/ development plan, with clear milestones to be achieved each year.
- To increase consistency of practice across a group of schools within a local authority, district, trust or network – for example, through peer review.

Ultimately, if you want to ensure that self-regulated learning permeates the entire school, it will be essential to have buy-in from the senior leadership team (SLT), including, most particularly, the commitment of the head teacher/principal.

Begin by reading this Facilitator Guide. You may want to look at the **FAMILIARISE** activities at the same time. Then explore the activities on the other **Professional Learning** cards and consider the rest of the **Leadership Learning** cards alongside these. As you do so, ask:

- How might we introduce **Activate** to staff so that it isn't seen as just a shiny new thing and is recognised as a positive developmental process?
- Do we want to engage in all the activities in the professional learning cycle in sequence, or would it be preferable for some staff to engage with different activities, depending on their experience or level of need? (NB: we do recommend that everyone begins with the **FAMILIARISE** activities.)
- How long would we want a professional learning cycle to last? Do we want it to run over a whole year, or would it be better over a single term or semester?
- How should we organise teams or groups to work with **Activate**? Should participation be on an opt-in basis or are we asking all staff to engage with it?
- How will we distribute the leadership of **Activate** through the school? (NB: we recommend that **Activate** is facilitated by colleagues who can champion the

resource, engaging with it alongside others and supporting them through the professional learning process.)

- What support or experiences will facilitators need before introducing **Activate** to their colleagues?
- Reflecting on the **Leadership Learning** cards, how will we create the conditions in school to ensure that colleagues can fully engage in the range of activities contained in the **Professional Learning** cards?
- The **EVALUATE** activities provide opportunities for reviewing the impact of **Activate**. How else might we evaluate the impact of **Activate** on the self-regulated learning of students, teachers and leaders?

Downloadable resources

Downloadable from www.crownhouse.co.uk/activate-resources.

- **Professional learning cycle**

  This one-page map summarises what is contained in each phase of the professional learning cycle and the resources needed.

- **Learning log**

  This can be used by individuals or groups of colleagues at any point in the professional learning cycle to reflect on their learning and think about next steps.

- **Self-regulated teaching and learning strategies**

  These are used with some of the **Teacher Action** and **Pupil Action** cards.

- **Developing self-regulated learning: action plan**

  This is designed as part of the **SHARE** phase to help teachers, leaders and support staff to embed changes to their practice in developing self-regulated learning.

- **The Activate theory of change**

  This **Leadership Learning** resource can be used in the **REFINE** phase. It explains the theory of change process and **Activate**'s theory of change in more detail than on page 8.

Annex 1
The Activate conceptual framework[1]

Teachers are not always clear about what the terms 'metacognition', 'self-regulation' and 'self-regulated learning' mean. This is not surprising, because education researchers are not always clear about what these terms mean either. Dinsmore et al. (2008: 392) reviewed 255 studies in an attempt to determine the 'core meaning of metacognition, self-regulation and self-regulated learning, as well as where these constructs converge and diverge'. This review found that only 49% of the studies provided explicit definitions, and that where this did happen, there were often key differences – as well as areas of overlap – in how these words are understood. As Schunk (2008: 465) wrote: 'these definitions have become diluted to the point where today we ask such questions as: Is metacognition part of self-regulation? Is self-regulated learning part of self-regulation? Is self-regulation more environmentally sensitive than metacognition, which is more of a personal factor?' Let's consider each in turn.

Metacognition

Metacognition is often referred to simply as 'thinking about thinking'. However, when the word was coined by the developmental psychologist John Flavell in 1976, it was conceived as a complex, dynamic process involving several moving parts. In 1979, Flavell published a short paper entitled 'Metacognition and cognitive monitoring', in which he suggested that children and young people learn to control their thinking by monitoring what they know about people (self and others), tasks and strategies. He proposed that this metacognitive knowledge grows through experience, by setting goals and by selecting strategies to achieve those goals. All of these components interact with one another, and through such interactions we develop metacognitive skills and further our metacognitive knowledge.

While it has great explanatory power, Flavell's model is too complex to be easily called to mind in the context of a busy lesson. Fortunately, others have provided simpler definitions. For example, Chris Watkins (2001: 1) defined metacognition succinctly as 'awareness of thinking processes, and "executive control" of such processes'. In **Activate**, we define metacognition even more simply:

Metacognition is monitoring and controlling your thought processes.

---

1   Some of the text in this annex has been adapted from J. Mannion (2018). Metacognition, self-regulation and self-regulated learning: what's the difference? *Impact* (12 September). Available at: https://my.chartered.college/impact_article/metacognition-self-regulation-and-self-regulated-learning-whats-the-difference/.

Self-regulation

Our understanding of self-regulation is largely based on the work of the psychologist Albert Bandura. In contrast to the cognitive, thought-based world of metacognition, Bandura viewed self-regulation as the process of influencing the external environment through our emotions and behaviours. However, the language used to describe self-regulation is very similar to that used to describe metacognition and, in a sense, the two can be seen as mirror images of one another. For example, Dinsmore et al. found that there was significant overlap in the language used to define the two terms, with two words cropping up far more than any others: *monitor* and *control*. Echoing Bandura, Dinsmore et al. (2008: 405) concluded that there is 'a clear cognitive orientation for metacognition, while self-regulation is as much concerned with human action as the thinking that engendered it'. In **Activate**, we define self-regulation as follows:

Self-regulation is monitoring and controlling your feelings and behaviours.

Please note: *we use the word 'feelings' because self-regulation relates to physical as well as emotional feelings.*

Self-regulated learning

Spanning the domains of thought processes, emotions and behaviours, it is clear that metacognition and self-regulation are broad concepts that extend beyond academic learning. As Fox and Riconscente (2008: 374) put it: 'understanding metacognition and self-regulation … requires situating them within the broad context of all activities for humans of all ages and points of development'.

Following the publication of Bandura's classic work *Social Foundations of Thought and Action* (1986), the concepts of metacognition and self-regulation were increasingly applied to the world of education. This led to the development of a new term: 'self-regulated learning'. Dale Schunk (2008: 465) describes self-regulated learning as 'the process whereby students activate and sustain *cognitions and behaviours* systematically oriented toward the attainment of their learning goals'.[2]

In **Activate**, we define self-regulation as follows:

Self-regulated learning is the application of metacognition and self-regulation to learning.

---

2   Our emphasis.

Annex 2
Powerful professional learning

Activate processes are based on research about professional development and learning approaches that lead to great teaching and learning, and how leadership can best support this (for example, Timperley et al., 2007; Jensen et al., 2016; Darling-Hammond et al., 2017; Cordingley et al., 2015 and 2020). Some key findings from this research base (Stoll et al., 2012) are summarised below.

Great professional learning:

- Starts with the end in mind. Professional learning comes out of considering the difference you want to make for pupils, which is also fundamental to our design theory of change.

- Challenges thinking as part of changing practice. You can only really know if this is happening if you talk to each other, which is why learning conversations are central to **Activate**.

- Is based on assessment of individual and school needs. It's important to know what each teacher needs to help them grow professionally, but if you want to ensure that all pupils and teachers in a school have the same opportunities to grow, you need to think about professional learning at the school and leadership level too.

- Connects work-based learning and external stimulation. External expertise (for example, research on self-regulated learning) is vital, but it has to connect to everyday practice, which is why the workplace is a key site for professional learning.

- Opportunities are varied, rich and sustainable. Professional learning isn't a quick fix. It needs to take place over time and, as for pupils, it needs to offer a range of high quality, different, ongoing learning experiences.

- Uses inquiry and action research as key tools. We now know that the most powerful forms of professional learning involve people in active inquiry (Timperley, 2011), investigating problems in pupil learning and wellbeing and exploring practices that can best enhance these.

- Is strongly enhanced through collaborative learning and joint practice development. A wide body of research highlights the benefits of social learning for adults as well as pupils.

- Is enhanced by creating professional learning communities within and between schools. Collaboration is part of the culture of schools where powerful professional learning occurs.

- Requires leadership to create the necessary conditions. The research findings are clear that leaders play a highly significant role in setting the context, promoting and participating in teachers' professional development (Robinson, 2011), and modelling professional learning by engaging in their own. This is a central design principle in **Activate** in that activities are included for both teachers and leaders.

Annex 3
Stimulating learning conversations

Learning conversations must be purposeful, intentionally exploring ways to engage learners, extend learning and make a difference (Figure 5). They need a focus, protocols and tools, and also facilitation. **Activate**'s focus is self-regulated learning and the external research base that underpins it. The **Activate** cards are the tools, containing protocols – frameworks and guidance – to help structure the conversations. Anyone can facilitate learning conversations. A key feature, though, is that in genuine learning conversations, everyone involved engages with curiosity. Diverse perspectives are welcomed, and you interrogate words, ideas and each other respectfully. You are willing to participate wholeheartedly – to be honest, to open up, surfacing what you know but don't always articulate, to listen to others, and to push yourself, or be pushed, to reflect deeply in ways that may challenge your thinking and prior understandings. Learning conversations often move you to a new place as you create new knowledge together that will underpin the changes you then decide to make to your practice.

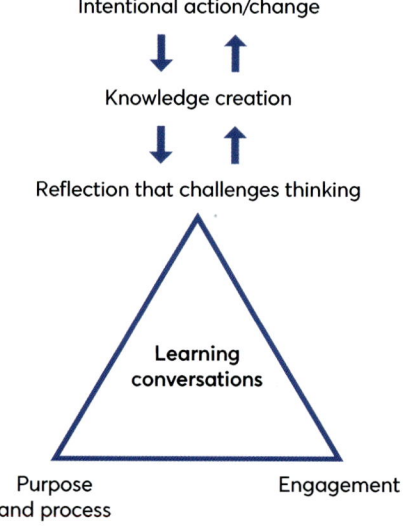

Figure 5. Learning conversations
Stoll (2012)

When participants' experience is blended with external expertise, it can deepen the conversation, stimulate reflection and challenge the status quo. The **Activate** cards and processes bring together your knowledge and experience with research knowledge about self-regulated learning (Figure 6). They are designed to help you to bring the self-regulated learning research knowledge to life in your own context and to fit your own specific needs.

*Figure 6. Bringing self-regulated learning research knowledge to life through **Activate***
Adapted from Stoll (2010) and NCSL (2006)

Through learning conversations everyone can develop clear and shared theories of change about how their own teaching for self-regulated learning, together with supportive leadership conditions, are intended to result in the ultimate outcome of self-regulated learners.

References and bibliography

Bandura, A. (1986). *Social Foundations of Thought and Action: A Social Cognitive Theory*. Englewood Cliffs, NJ: Prentice-Hall.

Cordingley, P., Higgins, S., Greany, T., Buckler, N., Coles-Jordan, D., Crisp, B., Saunders, L. and Coe, R. (2015). *Developing Great Teaching: Lessons from the International Reviews into Effective Professional Development*. London: Teacher Development Trust. Available at: https://tdtrust.org/wp-content/uploads/2015/10/DGT-Full-report.pdf.

Cordingley, P., Higgins, S., Greany, T., Crisp, B., Araviaki, E., Coe, R. and Johns, P. (2020). *Developing Great Leadership of CPDL*. CUREE, Durham University and the University of Nottingham. Available at: https://www.researchgate.net/publication/342658250_Developing_Great_Leadership_of_CPDL.

Darling-Hammond, L., Hyler, M. E. and Gardner, M. (2017). *Effective Teacher Professional Development*. Palo Alto, CA: Learning Policy Institute. Available at: https://learningpolicyinstitute.org/product/effective-teacher-professional-development-report.

Dinsmore, D. L., Alexander, P. A. and Loughlin, S. M. (2008). Focusing the conceptual lens on metacognition, self-regulation, and self-regulated learning. *Educational Psychology Review*, 20(4): 391–401.

Education Endowment Foundation (n.d.). *Teaching and Learning Toolkit*. London: Education Endowment Foundation. Available at: https://educationendowmentfoundation.org.uk/education-evidence/teaching-learning-toolkit.

Fisher, D., Frey, N. and Lapp, D. (2011). Coaching middle-level teachers to think aloud improves comprehension instruction and student reading achievement. *Teacher Educator*, 46(3): 231–243.

Flavell, J. H. (1976). Metacognitive aspects of problem-solving. In L. Resnick (ed), *The Nature of Intelligence*, pp. 231–235. Hillsdale, NJ: Erlbaum Associates.

Flavell, J. H. (1979). Metacognition and cognitive monitoring: a new area of cognitive–developmental inquiry. *American Psychologist*, 34(10): 906–911.

Fox, E. and Riconscente, M. (2008). Metacognition and self-regulation in James, Piaget, and Vygotsky. *Educational Psychology Review*, 20(4): 373–389.

Harries, E., Hodgson, L. and Noble, J. (2014). *Creating Your Theory of Change: NPC's Practical Guide*. London: New Philanthropy Capital. Available at: https://www.thinknpc.org/wp-content/uploads/2018/07/Creating-your-theory-of-change1.pdf.

Jensen, B., Sonnemann, J., Roberts-Hull, K. and Hunter, A. (2016). *Beyond PD: Teacher Professional Learning in High-Performing Systems*. Washington, DC: National Center on Education and the Economy. Available at: https://www.ncee.org/wp-content/uploads/2015/08/BeyondPDWeb.pdf.

Le Fevre, D., Timperley, H. and Ell, F. (2015). Curriculum and pedagogy: the future of professional learning and the development of adaptive expertise. In D. Wyse, L. Hayward, and J. Pandya (eds), *The SAGE Handbook of Curriculum, Pedagogy and Assessment*, pp. 309–324. Thousand Oaks, CA: Sage.

Le Fevre, D., Timperley, H., Twyford, K. and Ell, F. (2020). *Leading Powerful Professional Learning: Responding to Complexity with Adaptive Expertise*. Thousand Oaks, CA: Corwin.

Littleton, K. and Mercer, N. (2013). *Interthinking: Putting Talk to Work*. London: Routledge.

Mannion, J. (2018). Metacognition, self-regulation and self-regulated learning: what's the difference? *Impact* (12 September). Available at: https://my.chartered.college/impact_article/metacognition-self-regulation-and-self-regulated-learning-whats-the-difference/.

Mannion, J. and McAllister, K. (2020). *Fear is the Mind Killer: Why Learning to Learn Deserves Lesson Time – And How to Make it Work for Your Pupils*. Woodbridge: John Catt.

Mercer, N. (2008). *Three Kinds of Talk*. University of Cambridge: Thinking Together. Available at: https://thinkingtogether.educ.cam.ac.uk/resources/5_examples_of_talk_in_groups.pdf.

Mercer, N., Mannion, J. and Warwick, P. (2019). Oracy and dialogic education: the development of young people's spoken language skills. In N. Mercer, R. Wegerif and L. Major (eds), *The Routledge International Handbook of Research on Dialogic Education*, pp. 291–304. Abingdon and New York: Routledge.

Millard, W. and Menzies, L. (2016). *Oracy: The State of Speaking in Our Schools*. London: Voice 21 and LKMco. Available at: https://cfey.org/wp-content/uploads/2016/11/Oracy-Report-Final.pdf.

Minea-Pic, A., Nusche, D., Sinnema, C. and Stoll, L. (2021). *Teachers' Professional Learning Study: Diagnostic Report for the Flemish Community of Belgium*. OECD Policy Perspective No. 31. Paris: OECD. Available at: https://www.oecd.org/belgium/teachers-professional-learning-study-7a6d6736-en.htm.

NCSL (2006). Learning about learning networks. Nottingham: NCSL.

Ness, M. (2016). Learning from K-5 teachers who think aloud. *Journal of Research in Childhood Education*, 30(3): 282–292.

Porritt, V., Spence-Thomas, K. and Taylor, C. (2021). Leading professional learning and development. In T. Greany and P. Earley (eds), *School Leadership and Education System Reform*, 2nd edn, pp. 183–199. London: Bloomsbury.

Robinson, V. (2011). *Student-Centered Leadership*. San Francisco, CA: Jossey-Bass.

Schunk, D. H. (2008). Metacognition, self-regulation, and self-regulated learning: research recommendations. *Educational Psychology Review*, 20(4): 463–467.

Stoll, L. (2010). Connecting learning communities: capacity building for systemic change, in A. Hargreaves, A., Lieberman, M. Fullan and D. Hopkins (eds), *Second International Handbook of Educational Change*, pp. 469–484. Netherlands: Springer.

Stoll, L. (2011). Leading professional learning communities. In J. Robertson and H. Timperley (eds), *Leadership and Learning*, pp. 103–117. London: Sage.

Stoll, L. (2012). Stimulating learning conversations. *Professional Development Today*, 14(4): 6–12.

Stoll, L. (2020). Creating capacity for learning: are we there yet? *Journal of Educational Change*, 21(3): 421–430.

Stoll, L., Harris, A. and Handscomb, G. (2012). *Great Professional Development Which Leads to Great Pedagogy: Nine Claims from Research*. Nottingham: National College for School Leadership. Available at: https://assets.publishing.service.gov.uk/government/uploads/system/uploads/attachment_data/file/335707/Great-professional-development-which-leads-to-great-pedagogy-nine-claims-from-research.pdf.

Taplin, D. H. and Clark, H. (2012). *Theory of Change Basics: A Primer on Theory of Change*. New York: ActKnowledge. Available at: https://www.theoryofchange.org/wp-content/uploads/toco_library/pdf/ToCBasics.pdf.

Thinking Together (2019). *Ground Rules for Exploratory Talk*. Available at: https://thinkingtogether.educ.cam.ac.uk/resources/Ground_rules_for_Exploratory_Talk.pdf.

Timperley, H. (2011). *Realizing the Power of Professional Learning*. Maidenhead: Open University Press.

Timperley, H., Wilson, A., Barrar, H. and Fung, I. (2007). *Teacher Professional Learning and Development: Best Evidence Synthesis Iteration (BES)*. Wellington, New Zealand: Ministry of Education. Available at: https://www.educationcounts.govt.nz/publications/series/2515/15341.

Watkins, C. (2001). *Learning about Learning Enhances Performance*. Research Matters – No. 13. London: National School Improvement Network. Available at: https://discovery.ucl.ac.uk/id/eprint/10002803/1/Watkins2001Learning.pdf.

About the authors and organisations

Dr James Mannion is the director of Rethinking Education, an organisation dedicated to improving educational outcomes through implementation science, self-regulated learning and practitioner inquiry. He has a master's in person-centred education from the University of Sussex and a PhD in self-regulated learning from the University of Cambridge. James's doctoral thesis was an eight-year evaluation of the Learning Skills curriculum, a whole-school approach to teaching and learning that led to significant gains in subject learning across the curriculum, with accelerated gains among pupils from disadvantaged backgrounds. Much of the thinking that underpins the **Activate** conceptual framework is derived from James's doctoral work. Previously, James worked as a secondary school science teacher for 12 years and spent eight years in school leadership roles. He is an associate of the UCL Centre for Educational Leadership, which is part of IOE, UCL's Faculty of Education and Society; a founding fellow of the Chartered College of Teaching; and a by-fellow of Hughes Hall, University of Cambridge.

Dr Louise Stoll is Emeritus Professor of Professional Learning at the UCL Centre for Educational Leadership and an international consultant. Her work focuses on how schools, and local and national systems, create capacity for learning, with an emphasis on schools as learning organisations, professional learning communities, creative leadership, leadership development, and connecting research and practice. The author of many publications translated into six languages, she has also developed professional learning and leadership resources based on her research, including *Catalyst: An Evidence-Informed, Collaborative Professional Learning Resource for Teacher Leaders and Other Leaders Working Within and Across Schools* (Crown House Publishing, 2021) with Karen Spence-Thomas and other colleagues. Louise is involved in several initiatives focused on creative thinking in schools and is co-author of *Creative Thinking in Schools: A Leadership Playbook* (Crown House Publishing, 2023). She is a regular expert to the OECD, a former president of the International Congress for School Effectiveness and Improvement, and fellow of the Academy for the Social Sciences.

Karen Spence-Thomas MMus was a programme leader for bespoke leadership programmes in the UCL Centre for Educational Leadership. Previously a teacher and school leader in London, she specialised in designing and facilitating tailored professional development programmes within and across schools and other public sector organisations. She also co-led the IOE R&D network of schools. Her projects included: the Education Endowment Foundation-funded Research Learning Communities, the Economic and Social Research Council-funded Middle Leaders as Catalysts for Change (with Louise Stoll), the National College for Teaching and Leadership's research themes project (which she co-led), a teacher inquiry programme for Cognita schools worldwide, and a national school leadership development programme in Spain in partnership with EduCaixa (with Greg Ross). Among her publications is 'Leading professional learning and development', with Carol Taylor and Vivienne Porritt, in T. Greany and P. Earley (eds), *School Leadership and Education System Reform*, 2nd edn (Bloomsbury, 2021).

Greg Ross is an associate professor (teaching) at the UCL Centre for Educational Leadership. He specialises in the design and delivery of evidence-informed teacher and leadership development programmes for ministries of education, non-governmental organisations and international school groups. Greg also leads international consultancy projects focused on school system improvement and teaches on the Centre for Educational Leadership's postgraduate programmes. His current research focuses on the leadership of curriculum change in the Spanish school system. Projects Greg has recently led include: an annual year-long professional development programme for school leaders across Spain in partnership with EduCaixa; a peer review programme in Spain (also with EduCaixa); a teacher inquiry programme for Cognita schools worldwide; and the design of the IOE's International Professional Certificate in School Leadership (IPCSL), now offered worldwide. Before joining the IOE, Greg was a senior leader and English teacher in London schools. Prior to teaching, he worked on education and child rights programmes, and he has lived in Malawi, Cuba, Palestine and Lebanon.

Institute of Education

About the UCL Centre for Educational Leadership

Founded in 1826 in the heart of London, UCL is London's leading multidisciplinary university, with more than 16,000 staff and 50,000 students from over 150 different countries.

IOE, UCL's Faculty of Education and Society, has been consistently ranked number one for education for a decade in the QS World University Rankings by Subject.

The UCL Centre for Educational Leadership (CEL), located in the IOE, is the UK's largest university-based centre for research, teaching, development and innovation in educational leadership. It is a world-leading centre for knowledge creation, exchange and application to promote high-quality leadership, management and learning in education in London, the UK and internationally.

CEL provides research-informed advice and guidance for educational leaders, managers and policy makers, focused on the impact of their strategies and actions.

COGNITA

About Cognita

Cognita is a leading global system of over 100 individual yet interconnected schools, with a shared commitment to providing an outstanding holistic education that prepares students to thrive in a rapidly evolving world. We take our responsibility to educate and nurture each student very seriously, striving to ignite their passions and empowering them to make a difference in the world. Our ambition is for our students to have agency, adaptability and positive attitudes – we call this our A3.

We recognise that in education, there is no 'one size fits all' solution. We take pride in the diversity of our schools and our students, recognising that a tailored approach is required to adapt to local or individual needs. We facilitate global learning opportunities for our students and colleagues, encouraging a global mindset and sharing innovative ideas and expertise.

With 15,000 staff working across five regions, we are committed to providing the best possible education for our 75,000+ students. We are stronger together.

Acknowledgements

We are immensely grateful for the support we have received from many people during the inception, design, trialling, publication and promotion of **Activate**. With heartfelt thanks to:

- Our project partners at the global schools group, Cognita schools worldwide – especially Andy Hancock (education director, Asia), Esther Lum (education projects manager, Asia), Lydia Ching (senior project manager, Asia) and Jon Coward (school improvement partner, Europe).

- Colleagues at Cognita schools who provided invaluable feedback during the R&D phase – especially those from: St. Andrews International School, Sathorn (Thailand), El Limonar International School (Spain), Hastings School (Spain), St. Andrews International School, Dusit (Thailand), Polam School (UK), International School Ho Chi Minh City (Vietnam), St Clare's School (UK), Australian International School (Singapore), St. Andrews International School, Green Valley (Thailand), International School Ho Chi Minh City, American Academy (Vietnam), St. Andrews International School, Sukhumvit 107 (Thailand), Stamford American School (Hong Kong) and Hendon Preparatory School (UK).

- Colleagues from UK schools who trialled and provided invaluable feedback on the resource – especially Naheeda Maharasingam and Chantelle Daley (Rathfern Primary School), Harvey Eperon (Addey and Stanhope School), Kareen White and Micky Tumber (Capital City Academy), and Jo Gorman (Claremont Primary School).

- Our wonderful colleagues at the UCL Centre for Educational Leadership, IOE.

- David Bowman and the team at Crown House Publishing for their commitment and support in helping bring **Activate** to life.